Note to Educators and Parents

Reading is such an exciting adventure for young children! They are beginning to integrate their oral language skills with written language. To encourage children along the path to early literacy, books must be colorful, engaging, and interesting; they should invite the young reader to explore both the print and the pictures.

The *Animals I See at the Zoo* series is designed to help children read about the fascinating animals they might see at a zoo. In each book, young readers will learn interesting facts about the featured animal.

Each book is specially designed to support the young reader in the reading process. The familiar topics are appealing to young children and invite them to read — and re-read — again and again. The full-color photographs and enhanced text further support the student during the reading process.

In addition to serving as wonderful picture books in schools, libraries, homes, and other places where children learn to love reading, these books are specifically intended to be read within an instructional guided reading group. This small group setting allows beginning readers to work with a fluent adult model as they make meaning from the text. After children develop fluency with the text and content, the books can be read independently. Children and adults alike will find these books supportive, engaging, and fun!

— Susan Nations, M.Ed., author, literacy coach, and consultant in literacy development

I like to go to the zoo. I see **rhinos** at the zoo.

"Rhino" is short for rhinoceros. This word means "nose **horn**." Do you see the rhino's horn?

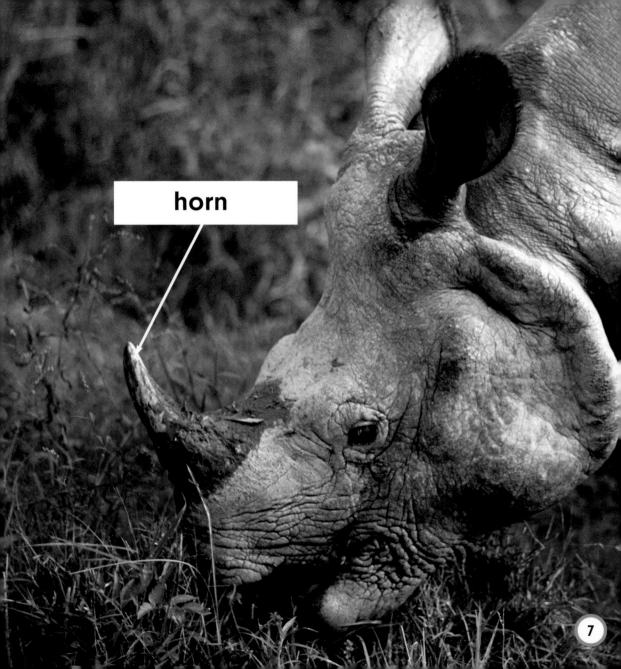

horn

Some rhinos
have one horn.
Some rhinos
have two horns.

horns

Rhinos use their horns to fight. When a rhino is in danger, it puts its head down and **charges**!

All rhinos are big. White rhinos are the biggest!

white rhino

13

All rhinos have tough skin. Some have smooth skin. Some have very **wrinkled** skin!

Rhinos like to
be near water.
Sometimes, they
take mud baths
to keep cool.

In the **wild**, rhinos eat grass and leaves. In the zoo, they eat hay, too.

I like to see rhinos at the zoo. Do you?

Glossary

charges — runs toward something at high speed

horn — a hard, pointed growth on the heads of some animals

rhinos — very large land animals with big bodies and short legs

wild — an animal's natural home

wrinkled — having a lot of folds, ridges, and crinkles

For More Information

Books

Hanson, Anders. *Rhino Horns*. Edina, Minnesota: ABDO, SandCastle, 2006.

Latta, Jan. *Rudy the Rhinoceros*. New York: Gareth Stevens, 2007.

Suen, Anastasia. *A Rhinoceros Grows Up*. Mankato, Minnesota: Coughlan Publishing, Picture Window Books, 2005.

Web Site

Zoobooks Virtual Zoo – Pet the Rhino

www.zoobooks.com/newFrontPage/animals/ virtualzoo/petrhino.htm

Learn about rhinos, take a rhino quiz, pet a rhino, and listen to the sounds a rhino makes.

Index

About the Author

Kathleen Pohl has written and edited many children's books, including animal tales, rhyming books, retold classics, and the forty-book series *Nature Close-Ups*. Most recently, she authored the Weekly Reader® leveled reader series *Let's Read About Animals* and *Where People Work*. She also served for many years as top editor of *Taste of Home* and *Country Woman* magazines. She and her husband, Bruce, share their home in the beautiful Wisconsin woods with six goats, a llama, and all kinds of wonderful woodland creatures.